Investing for Beginners

Cardinal Rules for Passive Income

Copyright 2016- Brian StClair
- All rights reserved.

This document is geared towards providing exact and reliable information in regards to the topic and issue covered. The publication is sold with the idea that the publisher is not required to render accounting, officially permitted, or otherwise, qualified services. If advice is necessary, legal or professional, a practiced individual in the profession should be ordered.

- From a Declaration of Principles which was accepted and approved equally by a Committee of the American Bar Association and a Committee of Publishers and Associations.

In no way is it legal to reproduce, duplicate, or transmit any part of this document in either electronic means or in printed format. Recording of this publication is strictly prohibited and any storage of this document is not allowed unless with written permission from the publisher. All rights reserved.

The information provided herein is stated to be truthful and consistent, in that any liability, in terms of inattention or otherwise, by any usage or abuse of any policies, processes, or directions contained within is the solitary and utter responsibility of the recipient reader. Under no circumstances will any legal responsibility or blame be held against the publisher for any reparation, damages, or monetary loss due to the information herein, either directly or indirectly.

Respective authors own all copyrights not held by the publisher.

Table of Contents

Introduction 5

Chapter 1: Going Over the Basics 6

Chapter 2: Have a Plan 11

Chapter 3: Be Smart When Trusting Others 21

Chapter 4: Be Logical, Not Emotional 27

Chapter 5: Diversity is Key 33

Chapter 6: Patience is a Virtue 37

Chapter 7: Common Pitfalls 42

Conclusion 47

Introduction

Hello, and thank you for purchasing this book. In this book, you will find the basic rules for a beginner to follow in investing. By now you probably know the basics, but you still probably are not at an advanced level as of yet. This book will guide you through the levels of what you need to know to become a great investor. I hope you find this book informational. Enjoy!

Chapter 1: Going Over the Basics

Investing is a tricky business. You can either get rich, or you can fall flat. However, with this book, you should be able to rise to the top fairly easily, as you learn everything you need to know about investing. But first, let us have a little refresher.

What is Investing

Investing is the process of buying something in hopes of selling it for way more money than you paid. It is a good deal for business savvy people who are great with numbers, and good at playing chicken with their finances. Investing is a very risky business, but it has its rewards, and the rewards are definitely worth the risk you put in.

How to Invest

There are many ways that you can invest. There is the ability to invest in stocks, options investing, and real estate investing to name a few. When you invest, you are spending a little bit of money in hopes of getting a return of a large amount of money. Investing is often at the hands of fate, but with a little guidance, you can steer the reins as much as possible, giving you a better shot at a successful investment. Let us take a look at the different types of investing.

Different Types of Investing

You can invest in the stock market, this is one of the most common types of investing. You do this by either investing in your retirement, or investing in a company.

When you invest in your retirement, the payout goes directly to you, and the money is yours to do with as you see fit. This is always good for when you decide to retire, as then you can be sure you have money to live off of for the rest of your years. You can either invest in a 401 K where you put your trust in a company that will match what you put in, however there are a bunch of rules, or an IRA where no one matches your money, but the interest goes up, and there are less rules.

One of the more popular ways to invest is to use a brokerage account to invest. This uses a third party to handle the particulars of investing for you. While it can be risky to let someone else handle your money, it is a lot less stress on you while you are making a profit.

Finally, there is a thing called DRIP. These are great if you want to invest in a long term kind of style, and there is no commissions to buy any. However, the ability to buy in is not always available, and there is often a minimum amount you have to reach.

There are many different ways to invest in stocks, those are just the main four, and the ones that are best for beginners. If you try to venture off too much without proper knowledge, then you can get into a heap of debt that you probably would rather avoid.

You can invest in options trading, where you buy an investment, but are not obligated to keep it, or even sell it. You can trade with others, and you can keep yours until the price goes up, and cash in. This is one of the most flexible types of investing, but can also be very risky.

Then there is real estate investing. It doesn't always have the millionaire turnout that the other two usually do, but it is one of the safest ways to invest, and it is the easiest type of investing. You literally just have to maintain properties, and they make the money for you. Plus it is literally a monthly income, without having to sell your asset. With stocks and options, you have to sell to make the money.

Why You Should Invest

Imagine living the lifestyle of your dreams. Imagine the mansion, or even just owning your own house. Imagine not having to worry about money, or anything for that matter. If you were able to do all of these things, would life be what you always dreamed it would be? You can have all of this and more with investing.

While investing can be pretty risky, it generally has a greater reward, and it can really bring in a lot of money. If you are wondering how much money investing can bring you, just look up any guru from wall street. You will see their fancy cars, and lush lifestyles, and you will realize that investing can bring you a lot of money.

You have to be willing to put in that risk, to gain the reward, which in the long run can be one of the best rewards you will ever have. Investing is like growing a garden. If you follow the right steps, and water it properly, then you may just have a great harvest that year, but if you neglect to learn about the crops you are sowing, you most likely will have a very bad harvest that year. You get out what you put in, if not more. But you have to actually put something in.

Investing is literally something anyone can do. You just have to have a bit of knowledge first. If you continue reading this book, it will give you helpful hints and tips on what to do when investing, and how to avoid making big mistakes.

Chapter 2:
Have a Plan

You can't go into a maze blind, and you can't make a cake without reading the directions first, so why would you try to wing it with your finances? You have to be able to figure out how to go about getting into the investing business. If you try to just do it without having a plan, you can end up going bankrupt, and losing everything. Not doing your research and not having a plan is one of the worst things that you could do when you are trying out investing.

If you do happen to luck out once, it probably wont happen again, so it is always best to have a plan, that you go through multiple times before finally enacting it, because the best plans are fool proof. It does not have to be elaborate, it just needs to be all inclusive. You have to plan for everything that can and will go wrong, otherwise you may find yourself in a heap of trouble.

If you do have a plan, your investment process will most likely go very smoothly, and you will find yourself successful. You won't get rich in a week, but over time, your investments will start to grow, and you will begin to make a profit. Once you make a profit, you can start investing a little bit of those profits as well to make even more money. But you won't get that far just by guesswork.

How to Make a Plan

The first thing you need to do is figure out how much money you can afford to invest. You do this by first figuring out how much money you need at the end of the year to feel like you succeeded. Then you decide how much money you have compared to that number. Say you had ten thousand dollars to invest, and you needed to bring in six thousand to feel good about yourself. That is what you need to figure out. What percentage do you need to bring back to feel like you accomplished something.

Then you have to decide what portions you are sending into a safe investment and what portions you are sending into risky investments. If you have ten thousand, and need to get six thousand back, you would be best off to put seven thousand into safe investments, and then you would put the remaining three into risky developments, if that is what you so desire. You have to decide exactly how much you are willing to lose with fees included, that way you don't put too much money into a risky investment, and forget the fees.

Figure out how much cost is accrued in the fees on your investments. There are several different types of fees depending on your type of investment. Like for stock market investing, you have brokerage fees, sale fees, expense ratios, and much more. There are similar fees in options trading as well. In real estate investing, there are agency fees, renovation fees, taxes, and many more expenses that are property specific. Always look into the fees you have to pay, otherwise you may find yourself more in the hole than you bargained for.

After you decide all of the monetary issues, you then have to decide where you are going to invest your money. This is important, because picking the wrong investment can be very detrimental to your bank account. If you pick the right investment, you may hit the pot of gold at the end of the rainbow. Taking what you decided on how much risk you can take with money, then you have to decide what company, stock, or option you are going to invest in. If you have ten thousand dollars, and wanna come home with six thousand of it, the best is to invest in a 401k or IRA with the six thousand, and then put three thousand into a risky stock, like flossing socks or something like that. Keep a thousand aside for fees, and to cushion the weight of the loss of stocks.

Once you invest, it is merely a matter of watching your stocks for any change in value. This is the most nerve-wracking time in investing. You have to literally watch your money decrease in value, or wait for it to increase in value. And during this time, your hands are tied. You can't get that money back until you sell the stocks, and if you sell them shortly after you invested them, they will go down seriously in value, and you will take a major hit to your finances.

Finally, you have to decide when you are going to sell your stocks. This is when you make your money. A good piece of advice is to wait until the value goes up three times, or a year has passed with no real change. You don't want to sell at the first sign of increase, because after the fees are paid, you won't be making a lot, if any, profit. You want to be patient, and let them get even higher before you sell. That way, if you didn't set aside money to pay for fees, you won't be taking a major hit on your finances.

After you sell your stocks, now it is time to decide if you want to reinvest. A lot of newbies to investing do not want to reinvest immediately, because they want to enjoy the money they made, this is not how passive income works. You don't truly make an income until you have bought and sold stocks for awhile, and are selling stocks monthly or more. The best idea, if you are trying to earn a real income from investing, is to reinvest as soon as possible. Follow your plan again, only change the place you invest your risky money.

There you go. A plan for investing in the stock market. If you are not quite sure yet of where you want to invest, you can do research on where to invest online. There are a few that are the best to invest in for beginners, such as:

Buffalo Wild Wings: This one is kind of expensive to buy into, but still not really. Even in this economy, there is always a want for beer and chicken wings, and you can get both here. This makes it a prime attraction for people, and buy buying into the stocks, you have a great chance of making a profit. The buy in is fifty eight dollars right now, but will eventually raise to around seventy as the franchise has plans to add over six hundred more restaurants, and the growth is slated to hit anywhere between fifteen and twenty five percent. You do not want to miss this.

Ancestry.com: I know it seems kind of weird to invest in a genealogy site, but I can guarantee you that you will not want to miss out on this opportunity. With rising popularity drawing more and more users to the site each year, the stocks are only rising. Well for now at least. Eventually the user rate will drop once people learn all that they can about their family history, but until then the stocks are raising thirty percent and the buy in is around thirty five dollars. Hold onto it for awhile and sell before the market drops, and you will be considered a stock master. Okay maybe not a master, but you will have made a smart decision.

Chemicals: These can be for cleaning, and much much more. The world will always need chemicals to perform even the most basic tasks. Investing in a company that creates useful chemicals is a great idea, because you know that your money is safe. Almost every chemical created has an important use, and puts it in high demand. The more demand there is, the higher your stock rate rises. This is what you need to make money.

Construction: There will always be things that need to be built. Especially with the continual rise in human population. We will always have to build new buildings, and other important structures. Investing in construction and construction materials is always a great idea, as they are always going to be around.

Solar Winds: This has nothing to do with solar or wind power. It is a software company that is starting out, but is already showing a good opportunity to deliver some promising results. Right now the buy in on average is around twenty three dollars. It doesn't get much better than that.

HMS Holding: This is a wonderful company to be a part of. They save Medicare patients hundreds of dollars in fraudulent payments (I.e double charges for a single medicine and things of that nature). However it is also showing potential for great returns. Shares are up twenty one percent from last year and the buy in is about twenty five dollars. This is one investment you will want to be a part of.

Electrical companies: Everyone uses electricity, and that is what makes it a good investment. Invest in a company that services multiple states for the best return on your investment. I believe that there may even be companies that service the globe. Investing in big companies will often get you a good return on your investment.

Wireless Communications: Let's face it. There is hardly a person in the world who doesn't own a cell phone, unless they live in an underdeveloped area, such as some parts of Kenya. Internet is wide spread now too. There are so many other types of wireless communications to invest in, and since this is only going to become a bigger market, investing in these companies is a great idea to make a lot of money.

There are many other companies that are good for investing in as well. Find what you are most interested in that will bring you a good return, and buy in. You will enjoy yourself knowing that your stocks are growing, and you are making money. These are good companies for a safe investment if you don't feel like putting all of your money into a retirement plan that you have to wait for years to access. You can sell whenever, but always remember to wait until it has increased enough to still make a decent sized profit after paying off fees.

Why You Really Need to Make a Plan

If you still are not convinced that you need to make a plan, then here are a few more reasons why making a plan is a good idea:

You are more likely to succeed: If you have a plan, you can follow it so that you know exactly what you need to do. If you are just winging it, it will be easier to over invest, and easier to make mistakes.

You have less stress: It is always more stressful when you go in without a plan. Especially when you are new. It makes it harder to figure out what you are supposed to do when you are going to invest, because you are new, and learning the information as you go. If you have a plan, you can research everything before you start to plan, and then you will be knowledgeable when you start investing.

You are able to see where your money will be headed, and a potential for profit growth when you make a plan. This is always a good motivator and will help keep you focused on your investment strategies as you continue on your investing path.

A plan will help with the basics of investing as you start to branch out into more risky areas, and learn more about investing in the markets that only the experts traverse in. When you can go back and follow the same steps, it becomes easier to adapt to more diverse areas, than if you are just winging it, because when you don't have a plan set out, you are struggling just to figure out what you are doing.

Convinced yet? Hopefully you are, because spending a couple hours building the perfect plan is a lot better than spending years rebuilding your finances from going into investing blindly. Having a plan is the difference between luxury and bankruptcy, between happiness and sadness, between success and failure. I could go on but I think you probably get the picture by now.

Chapter 3:
Be Smart When Trusting Others

Don't pay someone to lose your money. This is a cardinal rule in investing, because you want to earn money, not lose it. The easiest way to lose money is to trust the wrong person to be your broker. Just because you know them personally does not mean that they are skilled enough to handle your money in the investment world. They may have had a few successful investments, but there is more to it than enjoying success. They have to know what to do in case an investment loses money as well, and be skilled enough to at least help you break even. You can't always trust someone just because you like them, as that is what leads you like a lamb to slaughter.

When you go to investing, and you are new, it is a good idea to trust a broker until you learn enough to manage your own investments. However, do not trust any average Joe that you find on Facebook. Look for credentials. Go through an actual firm, rather than a person you know just because the fees are cheaper. While a firm will have higher fees, there will be a lot less risk of losing a lot of money due to the fact that they are professionally trained, and have a lot of experience in handling investments. A firm can make the process a lot easier for you as you learn more about investing.

Another good thing about investment broker firms is that they will assign you an agent, and this agent can walk you through the process and even teach you how to manage your own finances so that you will not need a broker in the future. However they are not forthcoming with the information, you have to ask a lot of questions to get them to fully walk you through everything because they do have a business to run, and they want your business as long as possible.

If you are going to trust another person with your money, it is pertinent that you have some proof that they know what they are doing. At least five years of experience in the field, an credentials to match. College degrees, training program certificates, and anything else they might have to prove that they know what they are doing. You can also ask to see their success rates against their failure rates, and use that to determine if they are trustworthy.

Trusting people these days is hard though. Even some firms have become scam artists. They charge so much in fees that it feels like they are robbing you at gunpoint for all of your profit. Always research the fees that an agency charges. Read the entire contract, fine print and all, before you sign anything, because once you sign there is no going back. This is where your finances can get in trouble, as the fees can literally drain any profit you may make and more.

The safest route to go is to learn to handle your finances yourself. If you would like to start out without a broker, don't invest until you have learned everything there is to know about investing in the market, and how to handle a situation if it goes wrong. This can take some time and a whole lot of research, but it is worth it to save some money while making good investments. If you are planning to go it alone as they say, you should definitely ask for advice from people who are well versed in investing at least. You may want to consult a financial advisor the first few times that you go to invest, at least until you feel comfortable enough to do it all alone. The goal here is to invest enough money to make a good chunk of profit, without losing your profit to fees. However, you can't just skip the fees and think that you will make a lot of money. There is a lot that goes into investing, and if you are not prepared for it, you can lose a lot of money.

Once you have decided whether you are going it alone, or if you are going to use a broker, then you can continue from there. If you are going to go with a broker then it is now time to find someone that you can trust. Ask around, and don't just choose the first broker you find. Find the best one for the type of investing you have chosen to get into. There are different broker agencies for different types of investing, and it is always best to research the different agencies that you are looking into so that you know which ones are best for which. Don't just go by their word. Look them up online, and read all the reviews about them. Often times there will be a mix of good and bad. They will be rated depending on their strengths in the investing areas. The bad reviews are their weaknesses, and the good reviews are their strengths. Always do your research.

Once you find a broker then you can start the investing process, but you really have to be sure you trust them first.

Why is Trusting the Right Person So Important?

You probably are not asking this question, I just really want to enforce the fact that you need to be careful in this day and age. Back twenty years ago, there was no problems with trusting your next door neighbor to watch your house for a weekend, leave a hundred dollars on the counter, and come back to that hundred dollars being in the same spot. Nowadays, it seems like you can't even trust your neighbors to look at your house without something being stolen.

It is the same way with your finances. You have to be careful because unlike twenty years ago, you can't trust somebody to tell you if they don't know what they are doing. Most people today would rather take advantage of you for their own personal gains than do the right thing and let you know you need to chose someone else.

When you trust the wrong person, you are literally trusting your lifestyle to someone who is going to take advantage of you, and that is not a good thing. Trusting the wrong person can literally destroy your finances, and force you into bankruptcy or worse. Brokers have access to all your information, so not only can they mess up on an investment, they can steal your identity if they are crooked enough, and you can't do anything to stop them other than change all of your information, or get them thrown in jail for identity theft. Both of those things are hard to do, and they really can cause a lot of problems in the long run.

That is why it is pertinent to always make sure that you are putting your trust in the right person. You can succeed only when you have the right people in your corner.

Chapter 4:
Be Logical, Not Emotional

As humans, we are predominantly emotional creatures, and that can be a great thing when we are expressing our love for someone, or choosing a puppy. However it is not great when it comes to deciding where your finances should go. Just because you get excited over the promise of a return does not always make it the best decision.

That is where logic comes in. You have to take a step back and analyze the situation before you can really make a decision. Otherwise your emotions will take over, and though they are good for some things, they will almost always lead you astray on things that have to do with your finances. You will be lured in by promises of large returns only to have all of your money stolen in a scam.

Just like with people you have to be careful of the companies you invest in. They may seem real, but some are scams that will take your money and run, because they are not real businesses. And if they put in the fine print that they are not a real business, then you can't sue them because you willingly gave up the money even though they provided you with the information that you were sending money to someone and it was not a real business.

You have to recondition yourself to not respond to emotional stimuli when entering your financial state of mind. You can be emotional in other areas of your life, but when it comes to finances, you need to be logical. Completely logical. However, do not always be suspicious of an investment. Merely cautious of investments that promise exorbitant returns. Those are generally the scams, because any legitimate investment does not promise any kind of return due to the fact that the stock market is always changing.

Being logical has many good effects in your investments, such as

- Safety from scams: You will be able to see right through a scam, and will know to avoid it. If you allowed your emotions to rule, you would be starry-eyed by any investment that promised thousands of dollars profit, and then get blindsided by them taking your money and running. If you are logical, then you will avoid these situations entirely, knowing that no investment is a pure promise of large returns, or any returns for that matter.

- Pros and cons: You can aptly weigh the pros and cons of investments and find out which one is right for you. This is important to do, because while an investment may seem promising, it may not have the stability that a lesser investment has. When you are clear and logical, you can think about every part of the investment. When you are allowing your emotions to take control, then you have issues with overlooking the bad parts and that can spell trouble for you.

- Logic saves the bank: If you are logical, your bank account will show the perks of that mindset. You will have a high success rate, and that means a lot of profit. Profit is what you are seeking, therefore logic will give you what you seek. You can relax knowing that you thought everything through before jumping into a risky investment. Emotion will blind you on fancy investments and you can lose a lot of money.

- You won't over invest: With logic you know exactly how much money that you can invest, and how much you need to put away for fees. This is important because if you invest too much and don't get a good enough return, then you can lose money when the fees hit. With emotion, it is super easy to over invest because you will be so excited about an investment that you want to get a lot of money back, so you put in more money than you can afford to in hopes of getting a major return.

- Your trust will be limited: You won't trust the wrong person with logic, because you know how important it is to get the most money you can from your investments. If you are logical, you will be able to research everyone you can to see who would be the best to handle your investment. If you fun by emotion, you may end up trusting a good friend to your money, when in reality he has no idea what he is doing. This is a bad idea, because it could mean that they lose all of your money, and still charge you for their services, and if you refuse to pay, then you could be taken to court, lose, and also have to pay court fees. Of course that is a worst case scenario, but it could still happen.

- You will make a plan: Logical people know that you need to have a well thought out plan to succeed in this business. A plan can help you figure out what you are going to invest on and how much money you are able to invest. If you invest this money well, then you can make a substantial profit, reinvest that profit, and let the trend continue. If you are ruled by emotion, then you will be more likely to try to go in without a plan, and that is where things can go awry. You need a plan to make sure you are going in the right direction with your finances.

These are some of the many reasons why logic is important when investing. If you are illogical, and run on emotion, then you can have a lot of problems down the road, and you will have financial issues as well. You have to think with logic rather than emotion in situations like these, as it will lead you on the right path.

Why is Logic so Important?

If you still don't feel like logic is that essential in investing, here are some things to think about. If you run on emotion, most of the time you refuse to even think about the bad things on something you like. It is the same reason that people fall in love with abusers. They refuse to acknowledge that there could be some bad things about them, and by the time they open their eyes it is too late. It is the same with finances. You become infatuated with a good deal, and ignore all the warning signs of a scam, or bad investment. You see them all around you but you don't want to acknowledge them. This can lead to you losing everything, even things you didn't put into the investments.

Logic is the one thing that makes investing successful. You will see all the pros and all the cons, and you won't be blinded by promises that an investment could not feasibly keep. You will see the fact that if it sounds to good to be true then it probably is, and you will steer clear of those issues. You need to remain logical, even in the face of a possible tremendous investment. Not so much that you turn down what really would be a good deal, but enough that you do not fall for a scam.

Chapter 5:
Diversity is Key

In investing, you need the best options to make the most profits, and you won't know which options are best if you do not branch out from your usual investments. You need to take control of the stocks you buy, and buy in to many different companies. This is important because the more diverse you are, the better chance of having multiple good investments that have a myriad of different returns.

Diversification starts when you start to take charge of the stocks you buy. If you are letting someone else make the choice for you, then you may not realize just how similar they are. You have to know everything about the stocks you buy into. What company are they for, what products or services does the company have, are there any similarities between the stocks you buy?

Diversity is important in investing just as it is in real life, because you have to have variety in your life to learn anything and to succeed. You need to know about every section of the game to really learn how it is played. Diversity allows you to know just which stocks are the best to invest in.

Sometimes you have to take a little hit, but it is worth it when you find the jack pot.

How to Diversify

- Look for similarities: If the stocks you buy have any similarities in common, then you are not very diverse in your buying. You need to have stocks from all ends of the spectrum. This means that sometimes you have to buy in to a company you aren't quite familiar with, because it is diverse and has great potential.

- Try to keep polar opposites on the board: When buying stocks, try to buy them in pairs of opposites. If you are buying into the oil fields, then also buy into the chocolate market. If you are buying into construction materials, then also buy into the floral market.

- Step out of your comfort zone: You have to step out of what you are comfortable in sometimes. This means investing in a company that you have no idea how it works. If you are not a tech person, that could mean investing in Microsoft You just have to get out there and do something that makes you feel like you are falling. With any luck you will fall into some decent profit.

- Find the perfect storm: If you are diverse enough, you will find the perfect storm of investment. You will have shares across the board, and the downfall of one company will be covered by the rising of another company. This is a great way to make sure that you always have an income with investing.

Why is Diversity so Important?

You are not only controlling the upside, you also have control of the downside as well. This is called controlling the risk. When you have a very diverse investment list, then if one company starts to go under, you still make a profit when another starts to rise. The more diverse you are, the less chance you have of taking a big hit when things go south with a company.

Most amateurs do not want to diversify, because they feel that if they stick with what works then they are in control of the risk. This is the farthest from the truth, as if their chosen market starts to go under they have nothing to offset the loss with, as every company they invest in is in the same market.

With diversification, you can control how you work your finances, because you can have a great balance of loss and profit, and you don't have to worry about what happens if your market goes down, because you have several others that will go up at the same time.

Chapter 6:
Patience is a Virtue

Investing is not a get rich quick business. That is something that you should know above all else. If you are looking to make an income immediately, and have a weekly check, then maybe a 9-5 job would be better for you. However, if you are willing to be patient, then investing can bring you profits that you never thought possible.

When you go to invest, sometimes you have to wait over a year to really make any money off of the investment. This does not mean that it is a bad investment, merely that it is a slow investment. You need to e patient, because sometimes the slow growers are the best returns you will have ever made.

Imagine this if you will. You are waiting for your date to show up in a bar. It is an hour past when he said he would be there, but you decide to wait it out. Finally he gets there, and he looks amazing. He is freshly showered, and his hair is perfect, as are his clothes. When he walks up to you he apologizes for being so late getting there. He discovered that his tire was flat and when he went to change it, he dropped his phone on the concrete and it shattered. He then pulls out the phone to show you. After he change the tire, he realized that he had gotten dirty, and would rather be late and look perfect than to show up looking dingy. He had hoped that you would still be there, despite his tardiness. You both order some drinks, and chat the night away, and you realize that this guy is really a catch. He is sweet, caring, funny, and smart. Flash forward to two years later, and he is down on one knee asking you to be his forever. If you had dipped out earlier, then you would have missed out on this wonderful guy, and your life would have taken a different turn. (If you are a guy, just switch it to girl from guy.)

It is the same with a slow to grow investment. If you have a low end stock, then it becomes almost like a clean slate, and it is often cheap. You can do so many things with it, and often times, when they explode, you had already bough a couple for cheap, so you have more profit than you know what to do with. You will be able to reinvest that money into another company, and make more profit off of that return. The cycle continues, and even though it is not always fast, you can get some great returns.

Also when investing, you have to be patient enough to wait for your stock to create the highest profit it possibly could before cashing in on it. If you sell it too early, you will not make as good of a profit as you would if you let its value build. This is something that a lot of new investors do not realize. If you sell at the first sign of profit, you will never get anywhere. Let it stew for awhile. Be patient, and allow it to make you real money, rather than chump change.

Why is Patience so Important?

You have to be patient to get anywhere in life. Have you ever heard the phrase "good things come to those who wait"? This is the truth. You have to be calm, and not let your emotions over rule you, as you wait for a sound return on your investment. Being impatient can lead to selling way before you have even given your investment a chance to make you the money it has the potential to, and if you sell that soon, then you can have some serious problems when it comes to paying fees, and making a profit. You may be lucky to break even.

Every rule in this book all boils down to patience. You have to be patient enough to do your research on investments and brokers. You have to be patient enough to make a plan. You have to be patient enough to find some diverse stocks to buy into. Patience is the basis of all of investing.

You cannot be impatient and expect to get anywhere in this business.

Patience can help you in many areas in investing, such as:

- Keeping you from selling out: As mentioned above, an impatient person has more of a chance of selling too soon than a patient person would. You can relax knowing that patience is all it takes to keep from losing money on an investment. Patience allows you to wait for the right moment to cash in on your investments, rather than cashing in too quickly.

- Keeps you vigilant: You will always be focused on your investment if you are patient. You will be able to pay attention to it, without getting so burnt out from paying too much attention to it. Rather than check it every second, you will check it regularly for any change, and can act then. An impatient person will check on it constantly for a little while, and then either sell it or forget about it until its too late to get the optimal return on it.

- Keeps you logical: If you are patient it is a lot easier to be logical, and that way you can think clearly about what you need to do, as you are looking into investing. This way you do not jump into something that is a bad idea head first. Instead you are patient enough to think everything through, and pay attention to what you have to do. You will make a plan, and not trust the wrong people. An impatient person often runs off of emotion, rather than logic, and this can create many problems in the investing business, as you trust the wrong people, and trust the wrong investments.

That is why patience is important. You cannot be an investor without patience, otherwise you will have a problem with maintaining profit.

Chapter 7: Common Pitfalls

There are many mistakes that new investors often make, and the purpose of this chapter is to make sure that you avoid them. Though there are a lot of quirky mistakes out there, this chapter will be focusing on the main ones, and discussing how to avoid them.

Going Blind/ Not Enough Research

You have to do your research when you are going into investing. You cannot go into it blind and expect to come out with any semblance of success. It just is not possible. If you go in blind, you will get so overwhelmed, and you will not know what to do. This can really cause problems when you are trying to make this your main source of income. You really need to take the time to do your research and to learn all that you can in this business. Especially if you are going to be managing your own finances, and not using a broker. If you are managing your own money to save money, you better be prepared to do some massive research because there is a lot to learn when it comes down to understanding investing.

Trusting the Wrong People

There is already a chapter about trusting the right people, and such, but that refers only to brokers. You also need to be sure that you can trust the people around you as well. Otherwise they can lead you astray in investing. Only ask advice from a trusted advisor. You cannot trust someone who has no idea what they are talking about when it comes to investing. Would you trust a stranger on the street to watch your child, or would you go to someone you know and ask them to watch the kid? The same goes with your finances. They should be like your children, and you should be as skeptical of people handling them as you are with your kids. People often will take advantage of you just to say that they can.

Expecting to Get Rich Quick

Many people expect to be rich by the end of the year in investments, because that is how the media portrays investing. The media is wrong. It can take years to make a sizable profit in this industry, and sometimes, you don't even make it to the millions. You often spend many years investing before you can finally retire, and live off of the money that you invested. You can't expect to own a yacht in six months with investing, and you can't expect to get anywhere if you feel like you aren't getting rich quick enough.

Quitting Your Day Job

For a few years, you will still need to continue working your regular job. This goes hand in hand with expecting to get rich quick. The reality is that you will not make enough money to support yourself in the beginning, and you will need a job to offset your expenses in investing, and to take care of keeping a roof over your heads, and food in your belly. You have to continue working your regular job, and make a regular paycheck before you can ever expect this gig to pay off. It can take many years before it does. Do you really want to be broke for years to come? If you continue working at your job, and profit you do make in the first year can help cover all the costs of living, and other expenses that you have in your life. You have to be prepared to work up until retirement. Then you when you cash in on all of your investments, then you will have a good amount of profit to live the rest of your years on.

Expecting Too Much

This is a common mistake that many people make. You expect to be great at investing the first time you try, and when you aren't you just give up. Investing is just like anything else. You have to work at it to make it into something worth doing. You can't just jump into it and become a success. It is like driving. Your first time in a vehicle you probably made a lot of mistakes, and you needed a lot of practice. Same with investing. You will make some mistakes, and you will need to try again. A lot. Once you learn the ropes though, it becomes a lot easier. You just have to stick with it.

Not Having a Clear Goal

Part of investing means having a goal you would like to reach. You need goals to give you a reason to keep striving for greatness. If you do not have goals, then you will become complacent, and start making mistakes in your investments. This can be financially destructive, and can be the death of your success. Goals can be about how much money you would like to make over all, or a certain time period to make a certain amount of money. If you do the second though, do not put ridiculous parameters on yourself. This is how you end up feeling like a failure and giving up. You want to give yourself a challenging goal, not an impossible one.

Forgetting Inflation

This is a big problem in today's investment society, because prices go up more than they ever have, and it is hard to guess what the prices of something will be in five years, let alone twenty years. However, many people don't even take into account inflation when they are going to invest. They do not set their goals for how much money they want to make high enough to cover their living costs in the future. Instead, they base their money on what they need now. That can cause problems when you finally cash in, only to find out that you don't have near enough money to live off of comfortably. Inflation is the number one killer of profit if you do not take it into account. Prices will always go up, so it is best to be prepared for it.

Conclusion

Thank you again for purchasing this book. I hope that you found it informational and instructional. Investing can be tricky, but hopefully this book helps you work through the process with ease, and sends you on your way to a more advanced outlook on the business.

If you liked this book, feel free to give it a good review. Thank you!

www.ingramcontent.com/pod-product-compliance
Lightning Source LLC
Chambersburg PA
CBHW070228210526
45169CB00023B/1268